MOVIE SONGS FOR TWO

Arrangements by Mark Phillips

ISBN 978-1-5400-3716-9

Visit Hal Leonard Online at
www.halleonard.com

Contact us:
Hal Leonard
7777 West Bluemound Road
Milwaukee, WI 53213
Email: info@halleonard.com

In Europe, contact:
Hal Leonard Europe Limited
42 Wigmore Street
Marylebone, London, W1U 2RN
Email: info@halleonardeurope.com

In Australia, contact:
Hal Leonard Australia Pty. Ltd.
4 Lentara Court
Cheltenham, Victoria, 3192 Australia
Email: info@halleonard.com.au

BABY ELEPHANT WALK

from the Paramount Picture HATARI!

CLARINETS

By HENRY MANCINI

Moderately, with humor

THE CANDY MAN

from WILLY WONKA AND THE CHOCOLATE FACTORY

CLARINETS

Words and Music by LESLIE BRICUSSE
and ANTHONY NEWLEY

CITY OF STARS

from LA LA LAND

Clarinets

Music by JUSTIN HURWITZ
Lyrics by BENJ PASEK and JUSTIN PAUL

CUPS
(When I'm Gone)
from the Motion Picture Soundtrack PITCH PERFECT

CLARINETS

Words and Music by A.P. CARTER,
LUISA GERSTEIN and HELOISE TUNSTALL-BEHRTENS

Moderately fast

FOOTLOOSE
Theme from the Paramount Motion Picture FOOTLOOSE

CLARINETS

Words by DEAN PITCHFORD
Music by KENNY LOGGINS

HALLELUJAH
featured in the DreamWorks Motion Picture SHREK

CLARINETS

Words and Music by
LEONARD COHEN

HAPPY

from DESPICABLE ME 2

Words and Music by
PHARRELL WILLIAMS

CLARINETS

I WILL ALWAYS LOVE YOU

featured in THE BODYGUARD

CLARINETS

Words and Music by
DOLLY PARTON

JAILHOUSE ROCK

from JAILHOUSE ROCK

Clarinets

Words and Music by JERRY LEIBER
and MIKE STOLLER

Moderately fast Rock

MIA & SEBASTIAN'S THEME

from LA LA LAND

CLARINETS

Music by JUSTIN HURWITZ

MRS. ROBINSON

from THE GRADUATE

CLARINETS

Words and Music by
PAUL SIMON

MOON RIVER

from the Paramount Picture BREAKFAST AT TIFFANY'S

Clarinets

Words by JOHNNY MERCER
Music by HENRY MANCINI

Moderately

THE PINK PANTHER

from THE PINK PANTHER

Clarinets

By HENRY MANCINI

Moderately, in 4

PUTTIN' ON THE RITZ

from the Motion Picture PUTTIN' ON THE RITZ
featured in YOUNG FRANKENSTEIN

CLARINETS

Words and Music by
IRVING BERLIN

THE RAINBOW CONNECTION
from THE MUPPET MOVIE

CLARINETS

Words and Music by PAUL WILLIAMS
and KENNETH L. ASCHER

RAINDROPS KEEP FALLIN' ON MY HEAD

from BUTCH CASSIDY AND THE SUNDANCE KID

CLARINETS

Lyrics by HAL DAVID
Music by BURT BACHARACH

ROCK AROUND THE CLOCK

featured in the Motion Picture AMERICAN GRAFFITI
featured in the Motion Picture BLACKBOARD JUNGLE

CLARINETS

Words and Music by MAX C. FREEDMAN
and JIMMY DeKNIGHT

SKYFALL

from the Motion Picture SKYFALL

CLARINETS

Words and Music by ADELE ADKINS
and PAUL EPWORTH

STAYIN' ALIVE

from the Motion Picture SATURDAY NIGHT FEVER

Clarinets

Words and Music by BARRY GIBB,
ROBIN GIBB and MAURICE GIBB

THAT'S AMORÉ
(That's Love)

from the Paramount Picture THE CADDY
featured in the Motion Picture MOONSTRUCK
featured in ENCHANTED

Words by JACK BROOKS
Music by HARRY WARREN

CLARINETS

TIME WARP
from THE ROCKY HORROR PICTURE SHOW

CLARINETS

Words and Music by
RICHARD O'BRIEN

UNCHAINED MELODY

from the Motion Picture UNCHAINED
featured in the Motion Picture GHOST

CLARINETS

Lyric by HY ZARET
Music by ALEX NORTH

YOU LIGHT UP MY LIFE

from YOU LIGHT UP MY LIFE

Clarinets

Words and Music by
JOSEPH BROOKS

HAL•LEONARD INSTRUMENTAL PLAY-ALONG

Your favorite songs are arranged just for solo instrumentalists with this outstanding series. Each book includes great full-accompaniment play-along audio so you can sound just like a pro! Check out www.halleonard.com to see all the titles available.

The Beatles

All You Need Is Love • Blackbird • Day Tripper • Eleanor Rigby • Get Back • Here, There and Everywhere • Hey Jude • I Will • Let It Be • Lucy in the Sky with Diamonds • Ob-La-Di, Ob-La-Da • Penny Lane • Something • Ticket to Ride • Yesterday.

_____	00225330	Flute	$14.99
_____	00225331	Clarinet	$14.99
_____	00225332	Alto Sax	$14.99
_____	00225333	Tenor Sax	$14.99
_____	00225334	Trumpet	$14.99
_____	00225335	Horn	$14.99
_____	00225336	Trombone	$14.99
_____	00225337	Violin	$14.99
_____	00225338	Viola	$14.99
_____	00225339	Cello	$14.99

Chart Hits

All About That Bass • All of Me • Happy • Radioactive • Roar • Say Something • Shake It Off • A Sky Full of Stars • Someone like You • Stay with Me • Thinking Out Loud • Uptown Funk.

_____	00146207	Flute	$12.99
_____	00146208	Clarinet	$12.99
_____	00146209	Alto Sax	$12.99
_____	00146210	Tenor Sax	$12.99
_____	00146211	Trumpet	$12.99
_____	00146212	Horn	$12.99
_____	00146213	Trombone	$12.99
_____	00146214	Violin	$12.99
_____	00146215	Viola	$12.99
_____	00146216	Cello	$12.99

Disney Greats

Arabian Nights • Hawaiian Roller Coaster Ride • It's a Small World • Look Through My Eyes • Yo Ho (A Pirate's Life for Me) • and more.

_____	00841934	Flute	$12.99
_____	00841935	Clarinet	$12.99
_____	00841936	Alto Sax	$12.99
_____	00841937	Tenor Sax	$12.95
_____	00841938	Trumpet	$12.99
_____	00841939	Horn	$12.99
_____	00841940	Trombone	$12.99
_____	00841941	Violin	$12.99
_____	00841942	Viola	$12.99
_____	00841943	Cello	$12.99
_____	00842078	Oboe	$12.99

The Greatest Showman

Come Alive • From Now On • The Greatest Show • A Million Dreams • Never Enough • The Other Side • Rewrite the Stars • This Is Me • Tightrope.

_____	00277389	Flute	$14.99
_____	00277390	Clarinet	$14.99
_____	00277391	Alto Sax	$14.99
_____	00277392	Tenor Sax	$14.99
_____	00277393	Trumpet	$14.99
_____	00277394	Horn	$14.99
_____	00277395	Trombone	$14.99
_____	00277396	Violin	$14.99
_____	00277397	Viola	$14.99
_____	00277398	Cello	$14.99

Movie and TV Music

The Avengers • Doctor Who XI • Downton Abbey • Game of Thrones • Guardians of the Galaxy • Hawaii Five-O • Married Life • Rey's Theme (from *Star Wars: The Force Awakens*) • The X-Files • and more.

_____	00261807	Flute	$12.99
_____	00261808	Clarinet	$12.99
_____	00261809	Alto Sax	$12.99
_____	00261810	Tenor Sax	$12.99
_____	00261811	Trumpet	$12.99
_____	00261812	Horn	$12.99
_____	00261813	Trombone	$12.99
_____	00261814	Violin	$12.99
_____	00261815	Viola	$12.99
_____	00261816	Cello	$12.99

12 Pop Hits

Believer • Can't Stop the Feeling • Despacito • It Ain't Me • Look What You Made Me Do • Million Reasons • Perfect • Send My Love (To Your New Lover) • Shape of You • Slow Hands • Too Good at Goodbyes • What About Us.

_____	00261790	Flute	$12.99
_____	00261791	Clarinet	$12.99
_____	00261792	Alto Sax	$12.99
_____	00261793	Tenor Sax	$12.99
_____	00261794	Trumpet	$12.99
_____	00261795	Horn	$12.99
_____	00261796	Trombone	$12.99
_____	00261797	Violin	$12.99
_____	00261798	Viola	$12.99
_____	00261799	Cello	$12.99

Songs from Frozen, Tangled and Enchanted

Do You Want to Build a Snowman? • For the First Time in Forever • Happy Working Song • I See the Light • In Summer • Let It Go • Mother Knows Best • That's How You Know • True Love's First Kiss • When Will My Life Begin • and more.

_____	00126921	Flute	$14.99
_____	00126922	Clarinet	$14.99
_____	00126923	Alto Sax	$14.99
_____	00126924	Tenor Sax	$14.99
_____	00126925	Trumpet	$14.99
_____	00126926	Horn	$14.99
_____	00126927	Trombone	$14.99
_____	00126928	Violin	$14.99
_____	00126929	Viola	$14.99
_____	00126930	Cello	$14.99

Top Hits

Adventure of a Lifetime • Budapest • Die a Happy Man • Ex's & Oh's • Fight Song • Hello • Let It Go • Love Yourself • One Call Away • Pillowtalk • Stitches • Writing's on the Wall.

_____	00171073	Flute	$12.99
_____	00171074	Clarinet	$12.99
_____	00171075	Alto Sax	$12.99
_____	00171106	Tenor Sax	$12.99
_____	00171107	Trumpet	$12.99
_____	00171108	Horn	$12.99
_____	00171109	Trombone	$12.99
_____	00171110	Violin	$12.99
_____	00171111	Viola	$12.99
_____	00171112	Cello	$12.99

Wicked

As Long As You're Mine • Dancing Through Life • Defying Gravity • For Good • I'm Not That Girl • Popular • The Wizard and I • and more.

_____	00842236	Flute	$12.99
_____	00842237	Clarinet	$12.99
_____	00842238	Alto Saxophone	$12.99
_____	00842239	Tenor Saxophone	$11.95
_____	00842240	Trumpet	$12.99
_____	00842241	Horn	$12.99
_____	00842242	Trombone	$12.99
_____	00842243	Violin	$12.99
_____	00842244	Viola	$12.99
_____	00842245	Cello	$12.99

HAL•LEONARD®